POEMS FOR THE
TIME CAPSULE

POEMS FOR THE TIME CAPSULE

Collected by
David Watts

WOLF RIDGE PRESS

ISBN   978-0-9818029-8-5
         0-9818029-8-2

Library of Congress Control Number: 2013912344

Book design by Jeremy Thornton, jftdesign.com
Cover photo "V838 Monocerotis Light Echo" coutersy of NASA, hubblesite.org

A deep bow to Joan Baranow for her expert editorial assistance.   .

WOLF RIDGE PRESS

350 Parnassus Avenue, Suite 900
San Francisco, CA 94117

www.wolfridgepress.com

Pre-publication version

for Joan

. . . . and those who love

and are loved by poetry

Forward

"Killer Poems," they've been called. Poems that knock your socks off, poems that detonate the "aha" moment of astonishment and wonder that accompanies a sudden revelation – poems of beauty and wisdom that change your life.

These are the high qualifications I've held for the poems collected in this anthology. It was not a conscious search. Mostly, the poem encounters me in some unsuspected way and knocks me off my feet. It is rare to come upon such an experience and rarer still to see, collected in one place, a community of poems sharing these qualities. Such an offering might be worthy material for a time capsule, a window backward from some distant future into a distilled essence of the past.

Poetry is critical to our existence. Built into our basic instincts is the impulse to turn to poems in times of need. In Persian culture, Hafiz brings guidance, for Judeo-Christians, the Bible. After 911, sales of poetry in the United States skyrocketed – this, in a culture where poetry is not center stage. Embedded in our genome is the trust that poetry brings a reliable source of clarity, wisdom, and guidance. We need it, as Robert Frost says, "not for answers but for a way through."

I have collected these poems over 30 years' experience writing, teaching, and publishing. They were kept in a pile on my desk intended simply for personal nourishment, not gathered for a book but to have available for study, reflection, inspiration. Each has withstood multiple readings, repeated dissections, and yet they never fail to stir that sense of recognition that comes when something significant has passed before us.

The book decided to publish itself, if only by the sheer force of chemistry that sparks from putting fine poems together in one place. The idea to collect the best of the best for a capsule for future generations finally jettisoned the book into existence. Blessings then, upon the boat that carries the effort forward.

So I share these jewels with you, happily, that you may build your own castles upon them, and so that we, as an evolving culture, may celebrate again and again, the best we have to offer.

May your castles have many rooms.

David Watts
Mill Valley, Summer, 2013

Contents

This Love
Ancient Egyptian 1

Four Quatrains
Rumi 2

Meditation at Lagunitas
Robert Hass 3

Morning Song
Sylvia Plath 4

Firescribbling
Tomas Tranströmer 5

Three Times My Life Has Opened
Jane Hirshfield 6

Seventh Eclogue
Miklós Radnóti 7

Love after Love
Derek Walcott 9

Sneezles
A. A. Milne 10

Son (part 1)
Len Roberts 12

Old Ice
Brenda Hillman 13

Whale Watch
Dean Young 14

Those Winter Sundays
Robert Hayden 20

The Lanyard
Billy Collins 21

The Lake Isle of Innisfree
William Butler Yeats 23

Miniature
Yannis Ritsos 24

Middle-Aged Woman at a Pond
Alicia Ostriker 25

At the Un-National Monument Along the Canadian Border
William Stafford 26

The Delights of the Door
Francis Ponge 27

The Secret
Denise Levertov 28

The Flute of Interior Time
Kabir 30

This is just to say
William Carlos Williams 31

The Guest
Anna Akhmatova 32

Fragment at the Beginning of Something
David Watts 33

Liddy's Orange
Sharon Olds 34

A Blessing
James Wright 35

There's a certain Slant of light
Emily Dickinson 36

Saint Francis and the Sow
Galway Kinnell 37

Prayer for Jackson
Amy Gerstler 37

Stopping by Woods on a Snowy Evening
Robert Frost 39

Ode to a Pair of Socks
Pablo Neruda 40

In the Middle of This Century
Yehuda Amichai 43

Two Poems
Lucille Clifton 45

Alone, Looking for Blossoms Along The River
Tu Fu 47

ancestors
harvey ellis 48

A Kite for Michael and Christopher
Seamus Heaney 50

Briefly It Enters, and Briefly Speaks
Jane Kenyon 51

To Autumn
John Keats 52

Train Ride
Ruth Stone 54

Do Not Go Gentle Into That Good Night
Dylan Thomas 55

Grand Canyon
Joan Baranow 56

The Green Plant
Wallace Stevens 57

Lovers
Stephen Dunn 58

The Gift
Li-Young Lee 59

Although there is not one moment
Ono no Komachi 61

Regarding Chainsaws
Hayden Carruth 62

Autumn Sonnet
May Sarton 66

Archaic Torso of Apollo
Rainer Maria Rilke 67

Last Night While I Was Sleeping
Antonio Machado 68

Saying Good-bye in a Ch'in-ling Wineshop
Li Po 69

Inscription for the Door
Eugene Ruggles 70

Frost at Midnight
Samuel Taylor Coleridge 71

Pied Beauty
Gerard Manley Hopkins 74

What lips my lips have kissed, and where and why
Edna St Vincent Millay 75

The Rose (part 1)
Theodore Roethke 76

Often I am Permitted to Return to a Meadow
Robert Duncan 77

Love Song (Lame)
Courtney Queeney 78

Fatness
Walter Pavlich 79

The Writer
Richard Wilbur 80

The Cloister
William Matthews 82

What the Doctor Said
Raymond Carver 83

A Green Crab's Shell
Mark Doty 84

may i feel said he
e. e. cummings 86

Barton Springs
Tony Hoagland 88

He Makes a House Call
John Stone 89

The Colonel
Carolyn Forché 91

Making Love After Long Absence
Nils Peterson 92

Four Haiku
Basho 93

The Neighborhood Dog
Russell Edson 94

Funeral Blues
W. H. Auden 96

What the Living Do
Marie Howe 97

"As We Are So Wonderfully Done with Each Other"
Kenneth Patchen 99

Jabberwocky
Lewis Carroll 100

The Bed by the Window
Robinson Jeffers 101

An Exercise in Love
Diane di Prima 102

You Who've Heard No News of Love
Hafiz 103

I began as a bloom of cotton
Lalla 105

How to Live on Bread and Music
Jennifer K. Sweeney 106

Acknowledgments 109

This Love

Ancient Egyptian circa 1200 BC

This love is as good
as oil and honey to the throat,
as linen to the body,
as fine garments to the gods,
as incense to the worshippers
when they enter in,
as the little seal-ring
to my finger.
It is like a ripe pear
in a man's hand,
it is like the dates
we mix with wine,
it is like the seeds
the baker adds to bread.
We will be together
even when old age comes.
And all the days in between
will be food set before us,
dates and honey, bread and wine.

Four Quatrains

36

When I am with you, we stay up all night.
When you're not here, I can't go to sleep.

Praise God for these two insomnias!
And the difference between them.

82

Today, like every other day, we wake up empty
and frightened. Don't open the door to the study
and begin reading. Take down a musical instrument.

Let the beauty we love be what we do.
There are hundreds of ways to kneel and kiss the ground.

388

I would love to kiss you.
The price of kissing is your life.

Now my loving is running toward my life shouting,
What a bargain, let's buy it.

914

Come to the orchard in Spring.
There is light and wine and sweethearts in the pomegranate flowers.
If you do not come, these do not matter.
If you do come, these do not matter.

Meditation at Lagunitas

All the new thinking is about loss.
In this it resembles all the old thinking.
The idea, for example, that each particular erases
the luminous clarity of a general idea. That the clown-
faced woodpecker probing the dead sculpted trunk
of that black birch is, by his presence,
some tragic falling off from a first world
of undivided light. Or the other notion that,
because there is in this world no one thing
to which the bramble of *blackberry* corresponds,
a word is elegy to what it signifies.
We talked about it late last night and in the voice
of my friend, there was a thin wire of grief, a tone
almost querulous. After a while I understood that,
talking this way, everything dissolves: *justice,*
pine, hair, woman, you and I. There was a woman
I made love to and I remembered how, holding
her small shoulders in my hands sometimes,
I felt a violent wonder at her presence
like a thirst for salt, for my childhood river
with its island willows, silly music from the pleasure boat,
muddy places where we caught the little orange-silver fish
called *pumpkinseed.* It hardly had to do with her.
Longing, we say, because desire is full
of endless distances. I must have been the same to her.
But I remember so much, the way her hands dismantled bread,
the thing her father said that hurt her, what
she dreamed. There are moments when the body is as numinous
as words, days that are the good flesh continuing.
Such tenderness, those afternoons and evenings,
saying *blackberry, blackberry, blackberry.*

Morning Song

Love set you going like a fat gold watch.
The midwife slapped your footsoles, and your bald cry
Took its place among the elements.

Our voices echo, magnifying your arrival. New statue.
In a drafty museum, your nakedness
Shadows our safety. We stand round blankly as walls.

I'm no more your mother
Than the cloud that distils a mirror to reflect its own slow
Effacement at the wind's hand.

All night your moth-breath
Flickers among the flat pink roses. I wake to listen:
A far sea moves in my ear.

One cry, and I stumble from bed, cow-heavy and floral
In my Victorian nightgown.
Your mouth opens clean as a cat's. The window square

Whitens and swallows its dull stars. And now you try
Your handful of notes;
The clear vowels rise like balloons.

Firescribbling

During the dismal months, my life sparkled only when I made love with you.
As the firefly ignites and then goes out, ignites, goes out – one can
    follow its flight by glimpses
in the dark night among the olive trees.

During the dismal months the soul sat shrunken and lifeless,
but the body took the straight path to you.
The night sky bellowed.
By stealth we milked the cosmos and survived.

Three Times My Life Has Opened

Three times my life has opened.
Once, into darkness and rain.
Once, into what the body carries at all times within it and starts
　　　to remember each time it enters the act of love.
Once, to the fire that holds all.
These three were not different.
You will recognize what I am saying or you will not.
But outside my window all day a maple has stepped from her leaves
　　　like a woman in love with winter, dropping the colored silks.
Neither are we different in what we know.
There is a door. It opens. Then it is closed. But a slip of light
　　　stays, like a scrap of unreadable paper left on the floor,
　　　or the one red leaf the snow releases in March.

The Seventh Eclogue

in the mountains above Zagubica. July 1944.

Evening approaches the barracks and the ferocious oak fence
braided with barbed wire, look, they dissolve in the twilight.
Slowly the eye thus abandons the bounds of our captivity
and only the mind, the mind is aware of the wire's tension.
Even fantasy finds no other path towards freedom.
Look, my beloved, dream, that lovely liberator,
releases our aching bodies. The captives set out for home.

Clad in rags and snoring, with shaven heads, the prisoners
fly from Serbia's blinded peaks to their fugitive homelands.
Fugitive homeland! Oh - is there still such a place?
still unharmed by bombs? as on the day we enlisted?
And will the groaning men to my right and my left return safely?
And is there a home where hexameters are appreciated?

Dimly groping line after line without punctuation,
here I write this poem as I live in the twilight:
inching, like blear-eyed caterpillar, my way on the paper;
torches and books have all been seized by the Lager guard,
mail has stopped and the fog from the mountains muffles the barracks.

Riddled with insects and rumours here in the mountains, Frenchmen,
Poles and dissident Serbs, loud Italians, dreamy Jews -
Fevered, a dismembered body, we lead a single existence,
waiting for news, a sweet word from a woman, and decency, freedom,
waiting for miracles, guessing the end obscured by the darkness.

Lying on boards, I am a captive beast among vermin,
the fleas renew their siege but the flies have at last retired.
Evening has come; my captivity, behold, is curtailed
by a day and so is my life. The camp is asleep. The moonshine
lights up the land and highlights the taut barbed wire fence,
drawing the shadows of armed prison guards, observed
    through the window,
walking, projected on walls, and spying the night's early noises.

Swish go the dreams, behold my beloved, the camp is asleep,
and the odd man who wakes with a snort turns about in his little space
and returns to his dreams at once, his face glowing. Alone
I sit up awake with the lingering taste of a cigarette butt
in my mouth instead of your kiss, and I get no merciful sleep,
for neither can I live nor die without you, my love, any longer.

Love after Love

The time will come
when, with elation,
you will greet yourself arriving
at your own door, in your own mirror,
and each will smile at the other's welcome,

and say, sit here. Eat.
You will love again the stranger who was your self.
Give wine. Give bread. Give back your heart
to itself, to the stranger who has loved you

all your life, whom you ignored
for another, who knows you by heart.
Take down the love letters from the bookshelf,

the photographs, the desperate notes,
peel your own image from the mirror.
Sit. Feast on your life.

Sneezles

Christopher Robin
Had wheezles
And sneezles,
They bundled him
Into
His bed.
They gave him what goes
With a cold in the nose,
And some more for a cold
In the head.
They wondered
If wheezles
Could turn
Into measles,
If sneezles
Would turn
Into mumps;
They examined his chest
For a rash,
And the rest
Of his body for swellings and lumps.
They sent for some doctors
In sneezles
And wheezles
To tell them what ought
To be done.
All sorts and conditions
Of famous physicians
Came hurrying round
At a run.
They all made a note
Of the state of his throat,

They asked if he suffered from thirst;
They asked if the sneezles
Came after the wheezles,
Or if the first sneezle
Came first.
They said, "If you teazle
A sneezle
Or wheezle,
A measle
May easily grow.
But humour or pleazle
The wheezle
Or sneezle,
The measle
Will certainly go."
They expounded the reazles
For sneezles
And wheezles,
The manner of measles
When new.
They said "If he freezles
In draughts and in breezles,
Then PHTHEEZLES
May even ensue."

Christopher Robin
Got up in the morning,
The sneezles had vanished away.
And the look in his eye
Seemed to say to the sky,
"Now, how to amuse them to-day?"

Son (part 1)

for Joshua L. Roberts

Walking the three tiers in first light, out
here so my two-year-old son won't wake the house,
I watch him pull and strip ragweed, chickory, yarrow,
so many other weeds and wildflowers
I don't know the names for, saying Big, and Mine,
and Joshua – words, words, words. Then
it is the moment, that split-second
when he takes my hand, gives it a tug,
and I feel his entire body-weight, his whole
heart-weight, pulling me toward
the gleaming flowers and weeds he loves.
That moment which is eternal and is gone in a second,
when he yanks me out of myself like some sleeper
from his dead-dream sleep into the blues and whites
and yellows I must bend down to see clearly, into the faultless
flesh of his soft hands, into his new brown eyes,
the miracle of him, and of the earth itself,
where he lives among the glitterings, and takes me.

Old Ice

The thought that you could even save the light,
that you could stop it from having to be
everywhere at once.

You stood in the ice cream shop
and from the street, in a group
of silly glass trumpets
light came,
and broke into millions of itself, shattered
from the pressure of being mute who knows how long.

There also, leaning against the counter
the child who saw nothing
but the bins of sweet color
separately rimmed with silver.

Behind you, thoughtfully placed by the owners, a photo
of an avalanche, its violence
locked in blue spears . . . The ice moved cruelly, one way only,
and behind the avalanche, and behind
the posts that held it,
the cars went back and forth like mediators.

You who do not exist:
you stared along the edges of the freezer:
frost glistened and clustered.
Suddenly it looked as if one act could be completed,
mounting over and over, even under terrible pressure.
Perhaps the tiny crystals would last forever.

Once it seemed the function of poetry
was to redeem our lives.
But it was not. It was to become
indistinguishable from them.

Whale Watch

Sometimes you may feel alone and crushed
by what you cannot accomplish
but the thought of failure is a fuzz
we cannot rid ourselves of
anymore than the clouds can their moisture.
Why would they want to anyway?
It is their identity and purpose
above the radish and radicchio fields.
Just because a thing can never be finished
doesn't mean it can't be done.
The most vibrant forms are emergent forms.
In winter, walk across a frozen lake
and listen to it boom and you will know
something of what I mean.
It may be necessary to go to Mexico.
Do not steal tombstones but if you do,
do not return them as it is sentimental
and the sentimental is a larval feeling
that bloats and bloats but never pupates.
Learn what you can of the coyote and shark.

Do not encourage small children
to play the trombone as the shortness
of their arms may prove quite frustrating,
imprinting a lifelong aversion to music
although in rare cases a sense of unreachability
may inspire operas of delicate auras.
If you hook, try to slice.
I have not the time to fully address
Spinoza but put Spinoza on your list.
Do not eat algae.
When someone across the table has a grain of rice
affixed to his nostril, instead of shouting,
Hey, you got rice hanging off your face!
thereby perturbing the mood
as he speaks of his mother one day in the basement,
brush your nose as he watches.
and hidden receptors in the brain
will cause him to brush his own nose
ergo freeing the stupid-looking-making rice.
There is so much to say and shut up about.

As regards the ever-present advice-dispensing susurration
of the dead, ignore it; they think everyone's
going to die. I have seen books with pink slips
marking vital passages
but this I do not recommend
as it makes the book appear foolish
like a dog in a sweater.
Do not confuse size with scale:
the cathedral may be very small,
the eyelash monumental.
Know yourself to be made mostly of water
with a trace of aluminum, a metal
commonly used in fuselages.
For flying, hollow bones are best or
no bones at all as in the honeybee.
Do not kill yourself.
Do not put the hammer in the crystal carafe
except as a performance piece.
When you are ready to marry,
you will know but if you don't,
don't worry. The bullfrog never marries,
ditto the space shuttle
yet each is able to deliver its payload:
i.e. baby bullfrogs and satellites, respectively.

When young, fall in and out of love like a window
that is open and only about a foot off the ground.
Occasionally land in lilacs
or roses if you must
but remember, the roses
have been landed in many times.
If you do not surprise yourself,
you won't surprise anyone else.
When the yo-yo "sleeps," give a little tug
and it will return unless it has "slept" too long.
Haiku should not be stored with sestinas
just as one should never randomly mix
the liquids and powders beneath the kitchen sink.
Sand is both the problem and the solution for the beach.
To impress his teacher, Pan-Shan lopped off
his own hand, but to the western mind,
this seems rather extreme.
Neatly typed, on-time themes
strongly spelled are generally enough.

Some suggest concentrating on one thing
for a whole life but narrowing down
seems less alluring than opening up
except in the case of the blue pencil
with which to make lines on one side
of the triangle so it appears to speed through the firmament.
Still, someone should read everything
Galsworthy wrote. Everyone knows
it's a race but no one's sure of the finish line.
You may want to fall to your knees
and beg for forgiveness without knowing precisely
for what. You may have a hole in your heart.
You may solve the equation but behind it
lurks another equation. You may never get
what you want and feel like you're already a ghost
and a failed ghost at that, unable to walk through walls.
There will be a purple hat. Ice cream.

You may almost ruin the wedding.
You may try to hang yourself but be saved
by a kid come home early from school
or you may be that kid who'll always remember
his mother that day in the basement,
how she seemed to know he'd done something wrong
before he even knew
and already forgave him,
the way she hugged him and cried.
Nothing escapes damage for long,
not the mountain or the sky.
You may be unable to say why
a certain song makes you cry until
it joins the other songs,
even the one that's always going on
and is never heard, the one that sings us into being.
On the phone, the doctor may tell you to come in.
It may rain for three days straight.
Already you've been forgiven,
given permission. Each week, cryptograms
come with the funny papers.
You're not alone.
You may see a whale.

Those Winter Sundays

Sundays too my father got up early
and put his clothes on in the blueblack cold,
then with cracked hands that ached
from labor in the weekday weather made
banked fires blaze. No one ever thanked him.

I'd wake and hear the cold splintering, breaking.
When the rooms were warm, he'd call,
and slowly I would rise and dress,
fearing the chronic angers of that house,

Speaking indifferently to him,
who had driven out the cold
and polished my good shoes as well.
What did I know, what did I know
of love's austere and lonely offices?

The Lanyard

The other day as I was ricocheting slowly
off the pale blue walls of this room,
bouncing from typewriter to piano,
from bookshelf to an envelope lying on the floor,
I found myself in the L section of the dictionary
where my eyes fell upon the word *lanyard*.

No cookie nibbled by a French novelist
could send one more suddenly into the past —
a past where I sat at a workbench at a camp
by a deep Adirondack lake
learning how to braid thin plastic strips
into a lanyard, a gift for my mother.

I had never seen anyone use a lanyard
or wear one, if that's what you did with them,
but that did not keep me from crossing
strand over strand again and again
until I had made a boxy
red and white lanyard for my mother.

She gave me life and milk from her breasts,
and I gave her a lanyard.
She nursed me in many a sickroom,
lifted teaspoons of medicine to my lips,
set cold face-cloths on my forehead,
and then led me out into the airy light

and taught me to walk and swim,
and I, in turn, presented her with a lanyard.
Here are thousands of meals, she said,
and here is clothing and a good education.
And here is your lanyard, I replied,
which I made with a little help from a counselor.

Here is a breathing body and a beating heart,
strong legs, bones and teeth,
and two clear eyes to read the world, she whispered,
and here, I said, is the lanyard I made at camp.
And here, I wish to say to her now,
is a smaller gift – not the archaic truth

that you can never repay your mother,
but the rueful admission that when she took
the two-tone lanyard from my hands,
I was as sure as a boy could be
that this useless, worthless thing I wove
out of boredom would be enough to make us even.

The Lake Isle of Innisfree

I will arise and go now, and go to Innisfree,
And a small cabin build there, of clay and wattles made:
Nine bean rows will I have there, a hive for the honey bee,
And live alone in the bee-loud glade.

And I shall have some peace there, for peace comes dropping slow,
Dropping from the veils of the morning to where the cricket sings;
There midnight's all a glimmer, and noon a purple glow,
And evening full of the linnet's wings.

I will arise and go now, for always night and day
I hear lake water lapping with low sounds by the shore;
While I stand on the roadway, or on the pavements gray,
I hear it in the deep heart's core.

Miniature

The woman stood up in front of the table. Her sad hands
begin to cut thin slices of lemon for tea
like yellow wheels for a very small carriage
made for a child's fairy tale. The young officer sitting opposite
is buried in the old armchair. He doesn't look at her.
He lights up his cigarette. His hand holding the match trembles,
throwing light on his tender chin and the teacup's handle. The clock
holds its heartbeat for a moment. Something has been postponed.
The moment has gone. It's too late now. Let's drink our tea.
Is it possible, then, for death to come in that kind of carriage?
To pass by and go away? And only this carriage to remain,
with its little yellow wheels of lemon
parked for so many years on a side street with unlit lamps,
and then a small song, a little mist, and then nothing?

Middle-Aged Woman at a Pond

The first of June, grasses already tall
In which I lie with a book. All afternoon a cardinal
Has thrown the darts of his song.

One lozenge of sun remains on the pond,
The high crowns of the beeches have been transformed
By a stinging honey. *Tell me,* I think.

Frogspawn floats in its translucent sacs.
Tadpoles rehearse their crawls.
There come the blackflies now,

And now the peepers. This is the nectar
In the bottom of the cup,
This blissfulness in which I strip and dive.

Let my questions stand unsolved
Like trees around a pond. Water's cold lick
Is a response. I swim across the ring of it.

At the Un-National Monument Along the Canadian Border

This is the field where the battle did not happen,
where the unknown soldier did not die.
This is the field where grass joined hands,
where no monument stands,
and the only heroic thing is the sky.

Birds fly here without any sound,
unfolding their wings across the open.
No people killed – or were killed – on this ground
hallowed by neglect and an air so tame
that people celebrate it by forgetting its name.

The Delights of the Door

Kings don't touch doors.

They don't know this joy: to push affectionately or fiercely before us one of those huge panels we know so well, then to turn back in order to replace it—holding a door in our arms.

The pleasure of grabbing one of those tall barriers to a room abdominally, by its porcelain knot; of this swift fighting, body-to-body, when, the forward motion for an instant halted, the eye opens and the whole body adjusts to its new surroundings.

But the body still keeps one friendly hand on the door, holding it open, then decisively pushes the door away, closing itself in—which the click of the powerful but well-oiled spring pleasantly confirms.

The Secret

Two girls discover
the secret of life
in a sudden line of
poetry.

I who don't know the
secret wrote
the line. They
told me

(through a third person)
they had found it
but not what it was
not even

what line it was. No doubt
by now, more than a week
later, they have forgotten
the secret,

the line, the name of
the poem. I love them
for finding what
I can't find,

and for loving me
for the line I wrote,
and for forgetting it
so that

a thousand times, till death
finds them, they may
discover it again, in other
lines

in other
happenings. And for
wanting to know it,
for

assuming there is
such a secret, yes,
for that
most of all.

The Flute of Interior Time

The flute of interior time is played whether we hear it or not.
What we mean by "love" is its sound coming in.
When love hits the farthest edge of excess, it reaches a wisdom.
And the fragrance of that knowledge!
It penetrates our thick bodies,
it goes through walls —
Its network of notes has a structure as if a million suns were arranged
        inside.
This tune has truth in it.
Where else have you heard a sound like this?

This is Just to Say

I have eaten
the plums
that were in
the icebox

and which
you were probably
saving
for breakfast

Forgive me
they were delicious
so sweet
and so cold

The Guest

Everything's just as it was: fine hard snow
beats against the dining room windows,
and I myself have not changed:
even so, a man came to call.

I asked him: "What do you want?"
He said, "To be with you in hell."
I laughed: "It seems you see
plenty of trouble ahead for us both."

But lifting his dry hand
he lightly touched the flowers.
"Tell me how they kiss you,
tell me how you kiss."

And his half-closed eyes
remained on my ring.
Not even the smallest muscle moved
in his serenely angry face.

Oh, I know it fills him with joy –
this hard and passionate certainty
that there is nothing he needs,
and nothing I can keep from him.

Fragment at the Beginning of Something. . .

My son brings me a stone and asks
which star it fell from,
he is serious
and so I must be careful, even though
I know he will place it
among those things that will leave him
someday, and he
will go on gathering. For this
is one of those moments
that turns suddenly towards you, opening
as it turns, as if for a moment
we paused on the edge
of a heart beat, conscious
of the fear that runs beside us
and how lovely it is to be with each other
in the long resilient mornings.

Liddy's Orange

The rind lies on the table where Liddy has left it
torn into pieces the size of petals and
curved like petals and rayed out like a
full-blown rose, one touch will make it come apart.
The lining of the rind is wet and chalky as
Devonshire cream, rich as the glaucous
lining of a boiled egg, all the protein
cupped in the ripped shell. And the navel,
torn out carefully,
lies there like a fat gold
bouquet, and the scar of the stem, picked out
with her nails, and still attached to the white
thorn of the central integument,
lies on the careful heap, a tool laid
down at the end of a ceremony.
All here speaks of ceremony,
the sheen of acrid juice, which is all that is
left of the flesh, the pieces lying in
profound order like natural order,
as if this simply happened, the way her
life at 13 looks like something that's just
happening, unless you see her
standing over it, delicately clawing it open.

A Blessing

Just off the highway to Rochester, Minnesota,
Twilight bounds softly forth on the grass.
And the eyes of those two Indian ponies
Darken with kindness.
They have come gladly out of the willows
To welcome my friend and me.
We step over the barbed wire into the pasture
Where they have been grazing all day, alone.
They ripple tensely, they can hardly contain their
       happiness
That we have come.
They bow shyly as wet swans. They love each other.
There is no loneliness like theirs.
At home once more,
They begin munching the young tufts of spring in the
       darkness.
I would like to hold the slenderer one in my arms,
For she has walked over to me
And nuzzled my left hand.
She is black and white,
Her mane falls wild on her forehead,
And the light breeze moves me to caress her long ear
That is delicate as the skin over a girl's wrist.
Suddenly I realize
That if I stepped out of my body I would break
Into blossom.

There's a certain Slant of light

There's a certain Slant of light,
Winter Afternoons –
That oppresses, like the Heft
Of Cathedral Tunes –

Heavenly Hurt, it gives us –
We can find no scar,
But internal difference,
Where the Meanings, are –

None may teach it – Any –
'Tis the Seal Despair –
An imperial affliction
Sent us of the Air –

When it comes, the Landscape listens –
Shadows – hold their breath –
When it goes, 'tis like the Distance
On the look of Death –

Saint Frances and the Sow

The bud
stands for all things,
even for those things that don't flower,
for everything flowers, from within, of self-blessing;
though sometimes it is necessary
to reteach a thing its loveliness,
to put a hand on its brow
of the flower
and retell it in words and in touch
it is lovely
until it flowers again from within, of self-blessing;
as Saint Francis
put his hand on the creased forehead
of the sow, and told her in words and in touch
blessings of earth on the sow, and the sow
began remembering all down her thick length,
from the earthen snout all the way
through the fodder and slops to the spiritual curl of the tail,
from the hard spininess spiked out from the spine
down through the great broken heart
to the sheer blue milken dreaminess spurting and shuddering
from the fourteen teats into the fourteen mouths sucking and
                blowing beneath them:
the long, perfect loveliness of sow.

Prayer for Jackson

Dear Lord, fire-eating custodian of my soul,
author of hermaphrodites, radishes,
and Arizona's rosy sandstone,
please protect this wet-cheeked baby
from disabling griefs. Help him sense when
to rise to his feet and make his desires known,
and when to hit the proverbial dirt. On nights
it pleases thee to keep him sleepless, summon
crickets, frogs and your chorus of nocturnal
birds so he won't conclude the earth's gone mute.
Make him astute as Egyptian labyrinths that keep
the deads' privacy inviolate. Give him his mother's
swimming ability. Make him so charismatic
that even pigeons flirt with him, in their nervous,
avian way. Grant him the clearmindedness
of a midwife who never winces when tickled.
Let him be adventurous as a menu of ox tongue hash,
lemon rind wine and pinecone Jell-O. Fill him with awe:
for the seasons, minarets' sawtoothed peaks,
the breathing of cathedrals, and all that lives –
for one radiant day or sixty pitiful years.
Bravely, he has ventured among us, disguised
as a newcomer, shedding remarkably few tears.

Stopping by Woods on a Snowy Evening

Whose woods these are I think I know.
His house is in the village, though;
He will not see me stopping here
To watch his woods fill up with snow.

My little horse must think it queer
To stop without a farmhouse near
Between the woods and frozen lake
The darkest evening of the year.

He gives his harness bells a shake
To ask if there is some mistake.
The only other sound's the sweep
Of easy wind and downy flake.

The woods are lovely, dark, and deep,
But I have promises to keep,
And miles to go before I sleep,
And miles to go before I sleep.

Ode to a pair of socks

Maru Mota brought me
a pair
of socks
that she knitted with her
shepherdess hands,
two socks soft
as rabbits.
I put my feet
into them
as into
two
cases
knitted
with threads of
twilight
and sheep's wool.

Wild socks,
my feet were
two wool
fish,
two big sharks
of ultramarine
crossed
by a golden braid,
two giant blackbirds,
two cannons:
my feet
were honored
in this way
by these

heavenly
socks.
They were
so beautiful
that for the first time
my feet seemed to me
unacceptable
like two decrepit
firemen, firemen
unworthy
of that
embroidered
fire,
of those shining
socks.

Anyway
I resisted
the sharp temptation
to save them
the way schoolboys
keep
lightning bugs,
the way scholars
collect
rare books,
I resisted
the mad impulse
to put them
in a golden
cage
and each day

to feed them birdseed
and the meat of a rosy melon.
Like explorers
in the forest
who give up the finest
young deer
to the roasting spit
and eat it
with regret,
I stretched out
my feet
and put on
the
lovely
socks
and then
my shoes.

And this is
the moral of my ode:
beauty is twice
beautiful
and goodness is doubly
good
when
it concerns two wool
socks
in winter.

In The Middle of This Century

In the middle of this century we turned to each other
with half faces and full eyes
like an ancient Egyptian picture
and for a short while.

I stroked your hair
in the opposite direction to your journey.
We called to each other,
like calling out the names of towns
where nobody stops
along the route.

Lovely is the world rising early to evil,
lovely is the world falling asleep to sin and pity,
in the mingling of ourselves, you and I,
lovely is the world.

The earth drinks men and their loves
like wine,
to forget.
It can't.
And like the contours of the Judean hills,
we shall never find peace.

In the middle of this century we turned to each other,
I saw your body, throwing shade, waiting for me,
the leather straps for a long journey
already tightening across my chest.
I spoke in praise of your mortal hips,
you spoke in praise of my passing face.

I stroked your hair in the direction of your journey,
I touched your flesh, prophet of your end,
I touched your hand, which has never slept,
I touched your mouth, which may yet sing.

Dust from the desert covered the table
at which we did not eat.
But with my finger I wrote on it
the letters of your name.

to my last period

well girl, goodbye,
after thirty-eight years.
thirty-eight years and you
never arrived
splendid in your red dress
without trouble for me
somewhere, somehow.

now it is done,
and I feel just like
the grandmothers who,
after the hussy has gone,
sit holding her photograph
and sighing, *wasn't she
beautiful? wasn't she beautiful?*

wishes for sons

i wish them cramps.
i wish them a strange town
and the last tampon.
i wish them no 7-11.

i wish them one week early
and wearing a white skirt.
i wish them one week late.

later i wish them hot flashes
and clots like you
wouldn't believe.   let the
flashes come when they
meet someone special.
let the clots come
when they want to.

let them think they have accepted
arrogance in the universe,
then bring them to gynecologists
not unlike themselves.

Alone, Looking for Blossoms Along the River

1.

The sorrow of riverside blossoms inexplicable,
And nowhere to complain—I've gone half crazy.

I look up our southern neighbor. But my friend in wine
Gone ten days drinking, I find only an empty bed.

2.

A thick frenzy of blossoms shrouding the riverside,
I stroll, listing dangerously, in full fear of spring.

Poems, wine—even this profusely driven, I endure.
Arrangements for this old, white-haired man can wait.

3.

A deep river, two or three houses in bamboo quiet,
And such goings-on: red blossoms glaring with white!

Among spring's vociferous glories, I too have my place:
With a lovely wine, bidding life's affairs *bon voyage*.

4.

Looking east to Shao, its smoke filled with blossoms,
I admire that stately Po-hua wineshop even more.

To empty golden wine cups, calling such beautiful
Dancing girls to embroidered mats—who could bear it?

5.

East of the river, before Abbot Huang's grave,
Spring is a frail splendor among gentle breezes.

In this crush of peach blossoms opening ownerless,
Shall I treasure light reds, or treasure them dark?

6.

At Madame Huang's house, blossoms fill the paths:
Thousands, tens of thousands haul the branches down.

And butterflies linger playfully – an unbroken
Dance floating to songs orioles sing at their ease,

7.

I don't so love blossoms I want to die. I'm afraid,
Once they are gone, of old age still more impetuous.

And they scatter gladly, by the branchful. Let's talk
Things over, little buds – open delicately, sparingly.

ancestors

my ancestors surround me
like walls of a canyon
quiet
stone hard
their ideas drift over me
like breezes at sunset

we gather sticks
and make settlements
what we do is only partly
our own
and partly continuation
down through the chromosomes

my son
my baby sleeps behind me
stirring in the night
for the touch
that lets him continue

he is arranging
in his small form the furniture
and windows of his home

it will be a lot like mine
it will be a lot like theirs

A Kite for Michael and Christopher

All through that Sunday afternoon
a kite flew above Sunday,
a tightened drumhead, a flitter of blown chaff.

I'd seen it grey and slippy in the making,
I'd tapped it when it dried out white and stiff,
I'd tied the bows of newspaper
along its six-foot tail.

But now it was far up like a small black lark
and now it dragged as if the bellied string
were a wet rope hauled upon
to lift a shoal.

My friend says that the human soul
is about the weight of a snipe,
yet the soul at anchor there,
the string that sags and ascends,
weighs like a furrow assumed into the heavens.

Before the kite plunges down into the wood
and this line goes useless
take in your two hands, boys, and feel
the strumming, rooted, long-tailed pull of grief.
You were born fit for it.
Stand in here in front of me
and take the strain.

Briefly It Enters, and Briefly Speaks

I am the blossom pressed in a book,
found again after two hundred years. . . .

I am the maker, the lover, and the keeper. . . .

When the young girl who starves
sits down to a table
she will sit beside me. . . .

I am food on the prisoner's plate. . . .

I am water rushing to the wellhead,
filling the pitcher until it spills. . . .

I am the patient gardener
of the dry and weedy garden. . . .

I am the stone step,
the latch, and the working hinge. . . .

I am the heart contracted by joy. . . .
the longest hair, white
before the rest. . . .

I am there in the basket of fruit
presented to the widow. . . .

I am the musk rose opening
unattended, the fern on the boggy summit. . . .

I am the one whose love
overcomes you, already with you
when you think to call my name. . . .

To Autumn

I

Season of mists and mellow fruitfulness,
    Close bosom-friend of the maturing sun;
Conspiring with him how to load and bless
    With fruit the vines that round the thatch-eves run;
To bend with apples the mossed cottage-trees,
    And fill all fruit with ripeness to the core;
        To swell the gourd, and plump the hazel shells
With a sweet kernel; to set budding more,
    And still more, later flowers for the bees,
    Until they think warm days will never cease,
        For Summer has o're-brimmed their clammy cells.

II

Who hath not seen thee oft amid thy store?
    Sometimes whoever seeks abroad may find
Thee sitting careless on a granary floor,
    Thy hair soft-lifted by the winnowing wind;
Or on a half-reaped furrow sound asleep,
    Drowsed with the fume of poppies, while thy hook
        Spares the next swath and all its twin'd flowers:
And sometimes like a gleaner thou dost keep
    Steady thy laden head across a brook;
    Or by a cider-press, with patient look,
        Thou watchest the last oozings hours by hours.

III

Where are the songs of Spring? Aye, where are they?
    Think not of them, thou hast thy music too, –
While barred clouds bloom the soft-dying day,
    And touch the stubble-plains with rosy hue;
Then in a wailful choir the small gnats mourn
    Among the river sallows, borne aloft
        Or sinking as the light wind lives or dies;
And full-grown lambs loud bleat from hilly bourn;
    Hedge-crickets sing; and now with treble soft
    The red-breast whistles from a garden-croft;
        And gathering swallows twitter in the skies.

Train Ride

All things come to an end;
small calves in Arkansas,
the bend of the muddy river.
Do all things come to an end?
No, they go on forever.
They go on forever, the swamp,
the vine-choked cypress, the oaks
rattling last year's leaves,
the thump of the rails, the kite,
the still white stilted heron.
All things come to an end.
The red clay bank, the spread hawk,
the bodies riding this train,
the stalled truck, pale sunlight, the talk;
the talk goes on forever,
the wide dry field of geese,
a man stopped near his porch
to watch. Release, release;
between cold death and a fever,
send what you will, I will listen.
All things come to an end.
No, they go on forever.

Do Not Go Gentle Into That Good Night

Do not go gentle into that good night,
Old age should burn and rave at the close of day;
Rage, rage against the dying of the light.

Though wise men at their end know dark is right,
Because their words had forked no lightning they
Do not go gentle into that good night.

Good men, the last wave by, crying how bright
Their frail deeds might have danced in a green bay,
Rage, rage against the dying of the light.

Wild men who caught and sang the sun in flight,
And learn, too late, they grieved it on its way,
Do not go gentle into that good night.

Grave men, near death, who see with blinding sight
Blind eyes could blaze like meteors and be gay,
Rage, rage against the dying of the light.

And you, my father, there on the sad height,
Curse, bless, me now with your fierce tears, I pray.
Do not go gentle into that good night.
Rage, rage against the dying of the light.

Grand Canyon

You have come to the edge in your t-shirt and tennis shoes,
the trail map snapping in the sudden wind, and there,

like nothing you had imagined, nothing
in the pocket-sized postcards or the traveler's guides,

is the split continent, enormous and jagged,
a terrible incision, terribly gorgeous,

the late afternoon air pouring in
like liquid spilled from far fissures or glacial thaw.

Below, invisible, is the green wiry river
rubbing against rock, pursuing its prehistoric task.

You'd not expected such a vast accident,
your shock the same as seeing a live heart

beating, or the blood of a baby's birth.
Soon you'll descend, shouldering a pack

down switchback trails into the open wound,
where, at dawn, you crawl from your nylon tent

to watch the sun, that rusty, iron ball,
hurl itself over the broken earth.

The Green Plant

Silence is a shape that has passed.
Otu-bre's lion-roses have turned to paper
And the shadows of the trees
Are like wrecked umbrellas.

The effete vocabulary of summer
No longer says anything.
The brown at the bottom of red
The orange far down in yellow,

Are falsifications from a sun
In a mirror, without heat,
In a constant secondariness,
A turning down toward finality –

Except that a green plant glares, as you look
At the legend of the maroon and olive forest,
Glares, outside of the legend, with the barbarous green
Of the harsh reality of which it is part.

Lovers

To keep the one you want
dig up a footprint of hers
and put it in a flowerpot.
Then plant a marigold, the flower
that doesn't fade.
And love her.
If she's distant now
it's for a reason beyond control.
So don't tamper with the impressions
left by her body when
for the last time
she leaves your bed.
Just smooth them out
and forget her.
Who is not vulnerable
to a stronger magic (the
broken glass, the bullets
in a yawn),
the terrible power of the one
less in love.

The Gift

To pull the metal splinter from my palm
my father recited a story in a low voice.
I watched his lovely face and not the blade.
Before the story ended, he'd removed
the iron sliver I thought I'd die from.

I can't remember the tale,
but hear his voice still, a well
of dark water, a prayer.
And I recall his hands,
two measures of tenderness
he laid against my face,
the flames of discipline
he raised above my head.

Had you entered that afternoon
you would have thought you saw a man
planting something in a boy's palm,
a silver tear, a tiny flame.
Had you followed that boy
you would have arrived here,
where I bend over my wife's right hand.

Look how I shave her thumbnail down
so carefully she feels no pain.
Watch as I lift the splinter out.
I was seven when my father
took my hand like this,

and I did not hold that shard
between my fingers and think,
Metal that will bury me,
christen it Little Assassin,
Ore Going Deep for My Heart.
And I did not lift up my wound and cry,
Death visited here!
I did what a child does
when he's given something to keep.
I kissed my father.

Although there is
not one moment
without longing,
still, how strangely
this autumn twilight fills me.

Regarding Chainsaws

The first chainsaw I owned was years ago,
an old yellow McCulloch that wouldn't start.
Bo Bremmer give it to me that was my friend,
though I've had enemies couldn't of done
no worse. I took it to Ward's over to Morrisville,
and no doubt they tinkered it as best they could,
but it still wouldn't start. One time later
I took it down to the last bolt and gasket
and put it together again, hoping somehow
I'd do something accidental-like that would
make it go, and then I yanked on it
450 times, as I figured afterwards,
and give myself a bursitis in the elbow
that went five years even after
Doc Arrowsmith shot it full of cortisone
and near killed me when he hit a nerve
dead on. Old Stan wanted that saw, wanted it bad.
Figured I was a greenhorn that didn't know
nothing and he could fix it. Well, I was,
you could say, being only forty at the time,
but a fair hand at tinkering. "Stan," I said,
"you're a neighbor. I like you. I wouldn't
sell that thing to nobody, except maybe
Vice-President Nixon." But Stan persisted.
He always did. One time we was loafing and
gabbing in his front dooryard, and he spied
that saw in the back of my pickup. He run
quick inside, then come out and stuck a double
sawbuck in my shirt pocket, and he grabbed
that saw and lugged it off. Next day, when I

drove past, I seen he had it snugged down tight
with a tow-chain on the bed of his old Dodge
Powerwagon, and he was yanking on it
with both hands. Two or three days after,
I asked him, "How you getting along with that
McCulloch, Stan?" "Well," he says, "I tooken
it down to scrap, and I buried it in three
separate places yonder on the upper side
of the potato piece. You can't be too careful,"
he says, "when you're disposing of a hex."
The next saw I had was a godawful ancient
Homelite that I give Dry Dryden thirty bucks for,
temperamental as a ram too, but I liked it.
It used to remind me of Dry and how he'd
clap that saw a couple times with the flat
of his double-blade axe to make it go
and how he honed the chain with a worn-down
file stuck in an old baseball. I worked
that saw for years. I put up forty-five
run them days each summer and fall to keep
my stoves het through the winter. I couldn't now.
It'd kill me. Of course they got these here
modern Swedish saws now that can take
all the worry out of it. What's the good
of that? Takes all the fun out too, don't it?
Why, I reckon. I mind when Gilles Boivin snagged
an old sap spout buried in a chunk of maple
and it tore up his mouth so bad he couldn't play
"Tea for Two" on his cornet in the town band
no more, and then when Toby Fox was holding

a beech limb that Rob Bowen was bucking up
and the saw skidded crossways and nipped off
one of Toby's fingers. Ain't that more like it?
Makes you know you're living. But mostly they wan't
dangerous, and the only thing they broke was your
back. Old Stan, he was a buller and a jammer
in his time, no two ways about that, but he
never sawed himself. Stan had the sugar
all his life, and he wan't always too careful
about his diet and the injections. He lost
all the feeling in his legs from the knees down.
One time he started up his Powerwagon
out in the barn, and his foot slipped off the clutch,
and she jumped forwards right through the wall
and into the manure pit. He just set there,
swearing like you could of heard it in St.
Johnsbury, till his wife come out and said,
"Stan, what's got into you?" "Missus," he says,
"ain't nothing got into me. Can't you see?
It's me that's got into this here pile of shit."
Not much later they took away one of his
legs, and six months after that they took
the other and left him sitting in his old chair
with a tank of oxygen to sip at whenever
he felt himself sinking. I remember that chair.
Stan reupholstered it with an old bearskin
that must of come down from his great-great-
grandfather and had the grit in it left over
from the Civil War and a bullet-hole as big
as a yawning cat. Stan latched the pieces together

with rawhide, cross fashion, but the stitches was
always breaking and coming undone. About then
I quit stopping by to see old Stan, and I
don't feel so good about that neither. But my mother
was having her strokes then. I figured
one person coming apart was as much
as a man can stand. Then Stan was taken away
to the nursing home, and then he died. I always
remember how he planted them pieces of spooked
McCulloch up above the potatoes. One time
I went up and dug, and I took the old
sprocket, all pitted and et away, and set it
on the windowsill right there next to the
butter mold. But I'm damned if I know why.

Autumn Sonnet

If I can let you go as trees let go
Their leaves, so casually, one by one;
If I can come to know what they do know,
That fall is the release, the consummation,
Then fear of time and the uncertain fruit
Would not distemper the great lucid skies
This strangest autumn, mellow and acute.
If I can take the dark with open eyes
And call it seasonal, not harsh or strange
(For love itself may need a time of sleep),
And treelike, stand unmoved before the change,
Lose what I lose to keep what I can keep,
The strong root, still alive under the snow,
Love will endure – if I can let you go.

Archaic Torso of Apollo

We cannot know his legendary head
with eyes like ripening fruit. And yet his torso
is still suffused with brilliance from inside,
like a lamp, in which his gaze, now turned to low,

gleams in all its power. Otherwise
the curved breast could not dazzle you so, nor could
a smile run through the placid hips and thighs
to that dark center where procreation flared.

Otherwise this stone would seem defaced
beneath the translucent cascade of the shoulders
and would not glisten like a wild beast's fur:

would not, from all the borders of itself,
burst like a star: for here there is no place
that does not see you. You must change your life.

Last Night While I Was Sleeping

Last night while I was sleeping
I dreamed–blessed illusion!–
a fountain flowed
inside my heart.
Water, tell me by what hidden
channel you came to me
with a spring of new life
I never drank?

Last night while I was sleeping
I dreamed–blessed illusion!–
I had a beehive
inside my heart,
and from my old bitterness
the gold bees
were contriving white combs
and sweet honey.

Last night while I was sleeping
I dreamed–blessed illusion!–
a fiery sun glowed
inside my heart.
It was fiery, giving off heat
from a red fireplace.
It was the sun throwing out light
and made one weep.

Last night while I was sleeping
I dreamed–blessed illusion!–
that it was God I held
inside my heart.

Saying Good-bye in a Ch'in-ling Wineshop

Spring winds perfume the shop
with heavy blooming catkins.

A girl from Wu pours wine
and encourages our drinking.

With friends from the city
I come to toast and say good-bye.

About to part, I point them toward
the great east-churning river.

Can any river possibly flow
beyond the love of friends?

Inscription for the Door

I have no enemies left,
only some friends who are late.
Come in, there is no lock, hang your coat
beside the fire and pull up a chair to its edge.
We shall drink tea and clear the path
leading back to the heart's first address.
You may have news. Tell me if our nations
revolve beside each other like seasons.
Why are those three strangers still kneeling
over their ashes? Invite them. Bring them in.
They can rest here beside this fire of meat.
Children sleep in the corners, taking notes.
A woman is dressing in the room overhead,
her footsteps are tablets I open to sleep.
The new wind is full of branches tonight,
leaving no holes in this darkness.
Around us, we can hear the dead sing.
Enter. I have no enemies left anymore,
only some friends who are late.

Frost at Midnight

The Frost performs its secret ministry,
Unhelped by any wind. The owlet's cry
Came loud – and hark, again! loud as before.
The inmates of my cottage, all at rest,
Have left me to that solitude, which suits
Abstruser musings: save that at my side
My cradled infant slumbers peacefully.
'Tis calm indeed! so calm, that it disturbs
And vexes meditation with its strange
And extreme silentness. Sea, hill, and wood,
This populous village! Sea, and hill, and wood,
With all the numberless goings-on of life,
Inaudible as dreams! the thin blue flame
Lies on my low-burnt fire, and quivers not;
Only that film, which fluttered on the grate,
Still flutters there, the sole unquiet thing.
Methinks, its motion in this hush of nature
Gives it dim sympathies with me who live,
Making it a companionable form,
Whose puny flaps and freaks the idling Spirit
By its own moods interprets, everywhere
Echo or mirror seeking of itself,
And makes a toy of Thought.

                    But O! how oft,
How oft, at school, with most believing mind,
Presageful, have I gazed upon the bars,
To watch that fluttering *stranger*! and as oft
With unclosed lids, already had I dreamt
Of my sweet birth-place, and the old church-tower,

Whose bells, the poor man's only music, rang
From morn to evening, all the hot Fair-day,
So sweetly, that they stirred and haunted me
With a wild pleasure, falling on mine ear
Most like articulate sounds of things to come!
So gazed I, till the soothing things, I dreamt,
Lulled me to sleep, and sleep prolonged my dreams!
And so I brooded all the following morn,
Awed by the stern preceptor's face, mine eye
Fixed with mock study on my swimming book:
Save if the door half opened, and I snatched
A hasty glance, and still my heart leaped up,
For still I hoped to see the *stranger's* face,
Townsman, or aunt, or sister more beloved,
My play-mate when we both were clothed alike!

     Dear Babe, that sleepest cradled by my side,
Whose gentle breathings, heard in this deep calm,
Fill up the interspersèd vacancies
And momentary pauses of the thought!
My babe so beautiful! it thrills my heart
With tender gladness, thus to look at thee,
And think that thou shalt learn far other lore,
And in far other scenes! For I was reared
In the great city, pent 'mid cloisters dim,
And saw nought lovely but the sky and stars.
But *thou*, my babe! shalt wander like a breeze
By lakes and sandy shores, beneath the crags
Of ancient mountain, and beneath the clouds,
Which image in their bulk both lakes and shores
And mountain crags: so shalt thou see and hear

The lovely shapes and sounds intelligible
Of that eternal language, which thy God
Utters, who from eternity doth teach
Himself in all, and all things in himself.
Great universal Teacher! he shall mould
Thy spirit, and by giving make it ask.

    Therefore all seasons shall be sweet to thee,
Whether the summer clothe the general earth
With greenness, or the redbreast sit and sing
Betwixt the tufts of snow on the bare branch
Of mossy apple-tree, while the nigh thatch
Smokes in the sun-thaw; whether the eave-drops fall
Heard only in the trances of the blast,
Or if the secret ministry of frost
Shall hang them up in silent icicles,
Quietly shining to the quiet Moon.

Pied Beauty

Glory be to God for dappled things –
   For skies of couple-colour as a brinded cow;
     For rose-moles all in stipple upon trout that swim;
Fresh-firecoal chestnut-falls; finches' wings;
   Landscape plotted and pieced – fold, fallow, and plough;
     And áll trádes, their gear and tackle and trim.

All things counter, original, spare, strange;
   Whatever is fickle, freckled (who knows how?)
     With swift, slow; sweet, sour; adazzle, dim;
He fathers-forth whose beauty is past change:
            Praise him.

What lips my lips have kissed, and where, and why

What lips my lips have kissed, and where, and why,
I have forgotten, and what arms have lain
Under my head till morning; but the rain
Is full of ghosts tonight, that tap and sigh
Upon the glass and listen for reply,
And in my heart there sirs a quiet pain
For unremembered lads that not again
Will turn to me at midnight with a cry.
Thus in the winter stands the lonely tree,
Nor knows what birds have vanished one by one,
Yet knows its boughs more silent than before:
I cannot say what loves have come and gone,
I only know that summer sang in me
A little while, that in me sings no more.

The Rose (part 1)

1.
There are those to whom place is unimportant,
But this place, where sea and fresh water meet,
Is important –
Where the hawks sway out into the wind,
Without a single wingbeat,
And the eagles sail low over the fir trees,
And the gulls cry against the crows
In the curved harbors,
And the tide rises up against the grass
Nibbled by sheep and rabbits.

A time for watching the tide,
For the heron's hieratic fishing,
For the sleepy cries of the towhee,
The morning birds gone, the twittering finches,
But still the flash of the kingfisher, the wingbeat of the scoter,
The sun a ball of fire coming down over the water,
The last geese crossing against the reflected afterlight,
The moon retreating into a vague cloud-shape
To the cries of the owl, the eerie whooper.
The old log subsides with the lessening waves,
And there is silence.

I sway outside myself
Into the darkening currents,
Into the small spillage of driftwood,
The waters swirling past the tiny headlands.
Was it here I wore a crown of birds for a moment
While on a far point of the rocks
The light heightened,
And below, in a mist out of nowhere,
The first rain gathered?

Often I Am Permitted to Return to a Meadow

as if it were a scene made-up by the mind,
that is not mine, but is a made place,

that is mine, it is so near to the heart,
an eternal pasture folded in all thought
so that there is a hall therein

that is a made place, created by light
wherefrom the shadows that are forms fall.

Wherefrom fall all architectures I am
I say are likenesses of the First Beloved
whose flowers are flames lit to the Lady.

She it is Queen Under The Hill
whose hosts are a disturbance of words within words
that is a field folded.

It is only a dream of the grass blowing
east against the source of the sun
in an hour before the sun's going down

whose secret we see in a children's game
of ring a round of roses told.

Often I am permitted to return to a meadow
as if it were a given property of the mind
that certain bounds hold against chaos,

that is a place of first permission,
everlasting omen of what is.

Love Song (Lame)

This is a little like high school
he said, when I wouldn't take off my clothes.
It was true, although in high school
I would've come over to torture him deliberately
and now the torture was an unfortunate side effect
of my sadness, and had nothing to do with him at all.
Sleeping with you would be like
a drowning woman grabbing an anvil,
I explained. A burning man guzzling gasoline.
Lame analogies, but I was trying to make a point.
When he got up for a drink, I missed him
but that feeling disappeared once he came back.
I sat there and tried to feel sad,
tracking my blue mute form
as it sank to a furrowed ocean floor.

Fatness

In the corner of the exercise yard,
Near the boxing ring,
In the short-breathed heat of July,
A shirtless man in prison jeans stoops
Down to feed his ration of turkey hash
To a twenty-eight pound cat.

It eats past fullness,
Stuffed fur mountain
Rubbing its appreciation on the knuckles
Of a man who shot his wife, his dog,
And his car before lunch.

He loves the beast in a fat way,
Because it pisses off voluntary jays,
Because it once backed up
And sprayed a lieutenant's pant leg,
Because it won't eat what it kills.

It is not just the walls they share.

He pets it for nothing, grimly.
It understands, purring freely.

The Writer

In her room at the prow of the house
Where light breaks, and the windows are tossed with linden,
My daughter is writing a story.

I pause in the stairwell, hearing
From her shut door a commotion of typewriter-keys
Like a chain hauled over a gunwale.

Young as she is, the stuff
Of her life is a great cargo, and some of it heavy:
I wish her a lucky passage.

But now it is she who pauses,
As if to reject my thought and its easy figure.
A stillness greatens, in which

The whole house seems to be thinking,
And then she is at it again with a bunched clamor
Of strokes, and again is silent.

I remember the dazed starling
Which was trapped in that very room, two years ago;
How we stole in, lifted a sash

And retreated, not to affright it;
And how for a helpless hour, through the crack of the door,
We watched the sleek, wild, dark,

And iridescent creature
Batter against the brilliance, drop like a glove
To the hard floor, or the desk-top,

And wait then, humped and bloody,
For the wits to try it again; and how our spirits
Rose when, suddenly sure,

It lifted off from a chair-back,
Beating a smooth course for the right window
And clearing the sill of the world.

It is always a matter, my darling,
Of life or death, as I had forgotten. I wish
What I wished you before, but harder.

The Cloister

The last light of a July evening drained
into the streets below. My love and I had hard
things to say and hear, and we sat over
wine, faltering, picking our words carefully.

The afternoon before I had lain across
my bed and my cat leapt up to lie
alongside me, purring and slowly
growing dozy. By this ritual I could

clear some clutter from my baroque brain.
And into that brief vacancy the image
of a horse cantered, coming straight to me,
and I knew it brought hard talk and hurt

and fear. How did we do? A medium job,
which is well above average. But because
she had opened her heart to me as far
as she did, I saw her fierce privacy,

like a gnarled, luxuriant tree all hung
with disappointments, and I knew
that to love her I must love the tree
and the nothing it cares for me.

What the Doctor Said

He said it doesn't look good
he said it looks bad in fact real bad
he said I counted thirty-two of them on one lung before
I quit counting them
I said I'm glad I wouldn't want to know
about any more being there than that
he said are you a religious man do you kneel down
in forest groves and let yourself ask for help
when you come to a waterfall
mist blowing against your face and arms
do you stop and ask for understanding at those moments
I said not yet but I intend to start today
he said I'm real sorry he said
I wish I had some other kind of news to give you
I said Amen and he said something else
I didn't catch and not knowing what else to do
and not wanting him to have to repeat it
and me to have to fully digest it
I just looked at him
for a minute and he looked back it was then
I jumped up and shook hands with this man who'd just given me
something no one else on earth had ever given me
I may even have thanked him habit being so strong

A Green Crab's Shell

Not, exactly, green:
closer to bronze
preserved in kind brine,

something retrieved
from a Greco-Roman wreck,
patinated and oddly

muscular. We cannot
know what his fantastic
legs were like —

though evidence
suggests eight
complexly folded

scuttling works
of armament, crowned
by the foreclaws'

gesture of menace
and power. A gull
gobbled the center,

leaving this chamber
— size of a demitasse —
open to reveal

a shocking, Giotto blue.
Though it smells
of seaweed and ruin,

this little traveling case
comes with such lavish lining!
Imagine breathing

surrounded by
the brilliant rinse
of summer's firmament.

What color is
the underside of skin?
Not so bad, to die,

if we could be opened
into *this* —
if the smallest chambers

of ourselves,
similarly,
revealed some sky.

may i feel said he

may i feel said he
(i'll squeal said she
just once said he)
it's fun said she

(may i touch said he
how much said she
a lot said he)
why not said she

(let's go said he
not too far said she
what's too far said he
where you are said she)

may i stay said he
(which way said she
like this said he
if you kiss said she

may i move said he
is it love said she)
if you're willing said he
(but you're killing said she

but it's life said he
but your wife said she
now said he)
ow said she

(tiptop said he
don't stop said she
oh no said he)
go slow said she

(cccome? said he
ummm said she)
you're divine! said he
(you are Mine said she)

Barton Springs

Oh life, how I loved your cold spring mornings
of putting my stuff in the green gym bag
and crossing wet grass to the southeast gate
to push my crumpled dollar through the slot.

When I get my allotted case of cancer,
let me swim ten more times at Barton Springs,
in the outdoor pool at 6 a.m., in the cold water
with the geezers and jocks.

With my head bald from radiation
and my chemotherapeutic weight loss
I will be sleek as a cheetah
—and I will not complain about life's

pedestrian hypocrisies;
I will not consider death a contractual violation.
Let my cancer be the slow-growing kind
so I will have all the time I need

to backstroke over the rocks and little fishes,
looking upwards through my bronze-tinted goggles
into the vaults and rafters of the oaks,
as the crows exchange their morning gossip

in the pale mutations of early light.
It was worth death to see you through these optic nerves,
to feel breeze through the fur on my arms,
to be chilled and stirred in your mortal martini.

In documents elsewhere I have already recorded
my complaints in some painstaking detail.
Now, because all things near water are joyful,
there might be time to catch up on praise.

He Makes a House Call

Six, seven years ago
when you began to begin to faint
I painted your leg with iodine

threaded the artery
with the needle and then the tube
pumped your heart with dye enough

to see the valve
almost closed with stone.
We were both under pressure.

Today, in your garden,
kneeling under the sticky fig tree
for tomatoes

I keep remembering your blood.
Seven, it was. I was just
beginning to learn the heart

inside out.
Afterward, your surgery
and the precise valve of steel

and plastic that still pops and clicks
inside like a ping-pong ball.
I should try

chewing tobacco sometimes
if only to see how it tastes.
There is a trace of it at the corner

of your leathery smile
which insists that I see inside
the house: someone named Bill I'm supposed

to know; the royal plastic soldier
whose body fills with whiskey
and marches on a music box

How Dry I Am;
the illuminated 3-D Christ who turns
into Mary from different angles;

the watery basement,
the pills you take, the ivy
that may grow around the ceiling

if it must. Here, you
are in charge – of figs, beans,
tomatoes, life.

At the hospital, a thousand times
I have heard your heart valve open, close.
I know how clumsy it is.

But health is whatever works
and for as long. I keep thinking
of seven years without a faint

on my way to the car
loaded with vegetables
I keep thinking of seven years ago

when you bled in my hands like a saint.

The Colonel

What you have heard is true. I was in his house. His wife carried a tray of coffee and sugar. His daughter filed her nails, his son went out for the night. There were daily papers, pet dogs, a pistol on the cushion beside him. The moon swung bare on its black cord over the house. On the television was a cop show. It was in English. Broken bottles were embedded in the walls around the house to scoop the kneecaps from a man's legs or cut his hands to lace. On the windows there were gratings like those in liquor stores. We had dinner, rack of lamb, good wine, a gold bell was on the table for calling the maid. The maid brought green mangoes, salt, a type of bread. I was asked how I enjoyed the country. There was a brief commercial in Spanish. His wife took everything away. There was some talk then of how difficult it had become to govern. The parrot said hello on the terrace. The colonel told it to shut up, and pushed himself from the table. My friend said to me with his eyes: say nothing. The colonel returned with a sack used to bring groceries home. He spilled many human ears on the table. They were like dried peach halves. There is no other way to say this. He took one of them in his hands, shook it in our faces, dropped it into a water glass. It came alive there. I am tired of fooling around he said. As for the rights of anyone, tell your people they can go fuck themselves. He swept the ears to the floor with his arm and held the last of his wine in the air. Something for your poetry, no? he said. Some of the ears on the floor caught this scrap of his voice. Some of the ears on the floor were pressed to the ground.

May 1978

Making Love after Long Absence

In a room perched on top of stairs
so narrow my shoulders could not
pass through two abreast, we found
ourselves together again. I had

forgotten how light the body is.
How it surrounds us like a cloud
in which the self can drift at its ease.
Far, far away were my diaphanous

feet and half as far my hands,
and just where I ended you began,
a thousand miles off yet close as breath
the moment lungs finish their brief

rest and begin to grow again. Augustine
says the body is the world's messenger to soul,
and soul gives shape again to what
she hears in her own kingdom.

So now, at the end of a day I've been
all talk, turning inward at last,
I can see you there swaying your breasts
in a grey blue lingering northern light.

Four Haiku

As the sound fades,
the scent of flowers comes up –
the evening bell.

❀

Having planted a banana tree,
I'm a little contemptuous
of the bush clover.

❀

Year after year
on the monkey's face
a monkey face

❀

This autumn –
why am I growing old?
bird disappearing among clouds.

The Neighborhood Dog

A neighborhood dog is climbing up the side of a house.

I don't like to see that, I don't like to see a dog like that, says someone passing in the neighborhood.

The dog seems to be making for that 2nd story window. Maybe he wants to get his paws on the sill; he may want to hang there and rest; his tongue throbbing from his open mouth.
Yet, in the room attached to that window (the one just mentioned) a woman is looking at a cedar box; this is of course where she keeps her hatchet: in that same box, the one in this room, the one she is looking at.

That person passing in the neighborhood says, that dog is making for that 2nd story window . . . this is a nice neighborhood, that dog is wrong . . .

If the dog gets his paws on the sill of the window, which is attached to the same room where the woman is opening her hatchet box, she may chop at his paws with that same hatchet. She might want to chop at something; it is, after all, getting close to chopping time . . .

Something is dreadful, I feel a sense of dread, says that same person passing in the neighborhood, it's that dog that's not right, not that way . . .

In the room attached to the window that the dog has been making for, the woman is beginning to see two white paws on the sill of that same window, which is attached to the same room where that same woman is beginning to see two white paws on the sill of that same window, which looks out over the neighborhood.

She says, it's wrong ... something ... the windowsill ... something ... the windowsill ...

She wants her hatchet. She thinks she's going to need it now ...

The person passing in the neighborhood says, something may happen ... That dog ... I feel a sense of dread ...

The woman goes to the hatchet in its box. She wants it. But it's gone bad. It's soft and nasty. It smells dead. She wants to get it out of its box (that same cedar box where she keeps it). But it bends and runs through her fingers ...

Now the dog is coming down, crouched low to the wall, backwards; leaving a wet streak with its tongue down the side of the house.

And that same person in the neighborhood says, that dog is wrong ... I don't like to see a dog get like that ...

Funeral Blues

Stop all the clocks, cut off the telephone.
Prevent the dog from barking with a juicy bone,
Silence the pianos and with muffled drum
Bring out the coffin, let the mourners come.

Let aeroplanes circle moaning overhead
Scribbling in the sky the message He Is Dead,
Put crêpe bows round the white necks of the public doves,
Let the traffic policemen wear black cotton gloves.

He was my North, my South, my East and West,
My working week and my Sunday rest,
My noon, my midnight, my talk, my song;
I thought that love would last for ever: I was wrong.

The stars are not wanted now: put out every one,
Pack up the moon and dismantle the sun;
Pour away the ocean and sweep up the wood;
For nothing now can ever come to any good.

What the Living Do

Johnny, the kitchen sink has been clogged for days, some utensil
    probably fell down there.
And the Drano won't work but smells dangerous, and the crusty dishes
    have piled up

waiting for the plumber I still haven't called. This is the everyday we
    spoke of.
It's winter again: the sky's a deep headstrong blue, and the sunlight
    pours through

the open living room windows because the heat's on too high in here, and
    I can't turn it off.
For weeks now, driving, or dropping a bag of groceries in the street,
    the bag breaking,

I've been thinking: This is what the living do. And yesterday, hurrying
    along those
wobbly bricks in the Cambridge sidewalk, spilling my coffee down my
    wrist and sleeve,

I thought it again, and again later, when buying a hairbrush: This is it.
Parking. Slamming the car door shut in the cold. What you called
    that yearning.

What you finally gave up. We want the spring to come and the winter to
    pass. We want
whoever to call or not call, a letter, a kiss—we want more and more and
    then more of it.

But there are moments, walking, when I catch a glimpse of myself in the
    window glass,
say, the window of the corner video store, and I'm gripped by a cherishing
    so deep

for my own blowing hair, chapped face, and unbuttoned coat that I'm
    speechless:
I am living, I remember you.

"As We Are So Wonderfully Done with Each Other"

As we are so wonderfully done with each other
We can walk into our separate sleep
On floors of music where the milkwhite cloak of childhood lies

O my lady, my fairest dear, my sweetest, loveliest one
Your lips have splashed my dull house with the speech of flowers
My hands are hallowed where they touched over your
     soft curving.

It is good to be weary from that brilliant work
It is being God to feel your breathing under me

A waterglass on the bureau fills with morning . . .
Don't let anyone in to wake us.

Jabberwocky

'Twas brillig, and the slithy toves
   Did gyre and gimble in the wabe;
All mimsy were the borogoves,
   And the mome raths outgrabe.

"Beware the Jabberwock, my son
   The jaws that bite, the claws that catch!
Beware the Jubjub bird, and shun
   The frumious Bandersnatch!»

He took his vorpal sword in hand;
   Long time the manxome foe he sought—
So rested he by the Tumtum tree,
   And stood awhile in thought.

And, as in uffish thought he stood,
   The Jabberwock, with eyes of flame,
Came whiffling through the tulgey wood,
   And burbled as it came!

One, two! One, two! And through and through
   The vorpal blade went snicker-snack!
He left it dead, and with its head
   He went galumphing back.

"And hast thou slain the Jabberwock?
   Come to my arms, my beamish boy!
O frabjous day! Callooh! Callay!"
   He chortled in his joy.

'Twas brillig, and the slithy toves
   Did gyre and gimble in the wabe;
All mimsy were the borogoves,
   And the mome raths outgrabe.

The Bed by the Window

I chose the bed downstairs by the sea-window for a good death-bed
When we built the house, it is ready waiting.
Unused unless by some guest in a twelvemonth, who hardly
      suspects
Its latter purpose. I often regard it,
With neither dislike nor desire; rather with both, so equaled
That they kill each other and a crystalline interest
Remains alone. We are safe to finish what we have to finish;
And then it will sound rather like music
When the patient daemon behind the screen of sea-rock and sky
Thrumps with his staff, and calls thrice: "Come, Jeffers."

An Exercise in Love

for Jackson Allen

My friend wears my scarf at his waist
I give him moonstones
He gives me shell & seaweeds
He comes from a distant city & I meet him
We will plant eggplants & celery together
He weaves me cloth

        Many have brought the gifts
        I use for his pleasure
        silk, & green hills
        & heron the color of dawn

My friend walks soft as a weaving on the wind
He backlights my dreams
He has built altars beside my bed
I awake in the smell of his hair & cannot remember
his name, or my own.

You Who've Heard No News of Love

You who've heard
no news of love
strive that you
may be master of this news

If you've not become
a traveler on this path
how can you prove
to be a guide?

In the school of perfect truths
try to please love's master
so your son may someday too
become a father

Sleeping and eating have left you
far below love's attainment
only when awake and hungry
can you reach love's heights

When God's love illumines
your heart and soul
you will be more brilliant
than the noonday sun

Wash your hands free
from the copper of this life
so you may gain love's alchemy
and be turned to gold

When from head to foot
only God's light remains
then footless and headless
on the path of Divine Majesty you will be

When you've been immersed in that Ocean
don't think for a moment
a single hair's been drenched
in any earthly sea

When you've attained
the vision of the Face
no doubt will remain
you ever held that vision

When above and below
the foundations of your life lie in ruins
don't think for a moment
you are bound by either

Hafiz! When desire for perfect union
enters your head
you'd best become dust
in the court of that Vision.

"I began as a bloom of cotton"

Dance, Lalla, with nothing on
but air. Sing, Lalla,
wearing the sky.

Look at this glowing day! What clothes
could be so beautiful, or
more sacred?

I began as a bloom of cotton,
outdoors. Then they brought me to a room
where they washed me. Then the hard strokes
of the carder's wife. Then another woman
spun thin threads, twisting me
around her wheel. Then the kicks
of the weaver's loom made cloth,
and on the washing stone, washermen
wet and slung me about
to their satisfaction, whitened me
with earth and bone,
and cleaned me to my own
amazement. Then the scissors
of the tailor, piece by piece,
and his careful finishing work.

Now at last, as clothes,
I find You and freedom.
This living is so difficult
before one takes your hand.

How to Live on Bread and Music

You need not confront the storm
though it comes with its guillotine
of wind and arrows of ice.
Let it come.
Take the wheat in your sage-rubbed hands
and pull out the dull chords.
Fold in Ravel. Hazelnuts.
Fold in the fury,
quarter notes rising from the grain.
These are your hands weighing the earth,
alchemy of salt and scale,
hum of clove bud.
Into the fire your life goes
to work its slow magic
and the song is the yeast
when the body wants
and it wants   fills   empties
as the day   fills   empties.
Song of milk glass.
Song of chaff.
That the thing delivers itself whole
like a blessing.
Feed the animal those brown fields.
Feed the rest of the body any tune,
any note will do.

Acknowledgments

"This Love" Ancient Egyptian, translated by Michael V. Fox with adaptations by Robert Hass from INTO THE GARDEN: A WEDDING ANTHOLOGY. Copyright © 1973 by Robert Hass and Stephen Mitchell reprinted by permission of Robert Hass.

"Four Quatrains" versions of Rumi from OPEN SECRET Threshold Books Copyright © 1984 by John Moyne and Coleman Barks reprinted by permission of Coleman Barks.

"Meditation at Lagunitas" by Robert Hass from PRAISE, The Ecco Press. Copyright © 1974, 1975, 1976, 1977, 1978, 1979 by Robert Hass, reprinted by permission of Robert Hass.

"Morning Poem" from ARIEL by Sylvia Plath. Copyright © 1961, 1962, 1963, 1964, 1965 by Ted Hughes permission pending from Harper and Row.

"Firescribbling" from THE WILD MARKET SQUARE by Tomas Transtromer, translated by John F. Deane. Copyright © John F. Deane reprinted by permission of Dedalus Press.

"Three Times My Life Has Opened" by Jane Hirshfield from THE LIVES OF THE HEART, Harper Perennial. Copyright © 1997 by Jane Hirshfield. Reprinted by permission of Jane Hirshfield.

"Seventh Eclogue" by Miklós Radnóti, translated by Thomas Land first appeared in Pennine Platform, published here with permission of the editor, Nicholas Bielby and also the translator, Thomas Land.

"Love After Love" from COLLECTED POEMS 1948-1984 by Derek Walcott. Copyright © 1986 by Derek Walcott. Reprinted by permission of Farrar, Straus and Giroux, LLC.

"Sneezles" from The Complete Poems of Winnie-the-Pooh. Copyright © The Trustees of the Pooh Properties, permission pending from Curtis Brown Limited, London.

"Son (Part 1)" from SWEET ONES by Len Roberts. Copyright © 1988 by Len Roberts, permission from Milkweed Editions.

"Old Ice" by Brenda Hillman from BRIGHT EXISTENCE, Wesleyan University Press. Copyright © 1993, reprinted by permission of Brenda Hillman.

"Whale Watch" by Dean Young from SKID, University of Pittsburgh Press. Copyright © 2002 by Dean Young, reprinted by permission of Dean Young.

"Those Winter Sundays". Copyright © 1966 by Robert Hayden, from ANGLE OF ASCENT: New and Selected Poems by Robert Hayden. Used by permission of Liveright Publishing Corporation.

"The Lanyard" from THE TROUBLE WITH POETRY by Billy Collins. Copyright © 2005 by Billy Collins, permission from Random House.